# Alien Garden Monsters

By Aina Taurina

...

...

You are very welcome in my world of flowers, trees, bushes, meadows, pots, birds, snails, insects, etc.

Many plants were in this garden before I moved in, so I needed to find their names. It looks like the Flowering Currant, however its flowers are pink. If they were redder it could be Ribes sanguineum "King Edward VII"

. Yes, there it is, a snail, my most unwanted garden guest. However, there are many plants that snails don't fancy to eat, so I am on the way to garden that way. Sorry snails, no late supper for you. You can lick that casting-iron stake. Cheers!

Colours are any garden's jewels, so there is not a boring day in the garden all year around. Even snow makes an interesting difference in the mild England's climate. Usually it does not make any harm and melts away very fast. But I was lucky enough to take some photos of my garden's disasters under snow.

This lovely Hart's Tongue Fern survived last winter's white surprise. In the spring I just cut off brown leaves and it made a perfect regrow. And, yes, it feels good in a pot on the fence, away from direct sunlight.

Any garden needs some predators to keep it free from pests. I would be happy to have a real one. Anyway, this Gecko is beautiful and, who knows, maybe under special circumstances, for example, in a full Moon's night it becomes alive. You never know what little monsters are capable for.

 Wow...there is one more scary monster, the Dragon. I love it.

It is not always easy to find names of plants that were planted before I came here. This rose is very tall (but it is not a climbing rose) with a beautiful scent and only in my third attempt I was successful to root a couple of cuttings. They wait in a propagator for the spring and permanent place to grow and make the garden even more beautiful.

Often I simply walk around the garden and take photos. Again, I don't know that beauty's name, however, I was surprised to find that yellow roses have different meanings among nations and how those meanings were changed during centuries.

For example, in China a yellow rose is never given to an alive person, because it is a symbol of death. However, in India a yellow rose represents passion. But in Victorian times with yellow rose you could express jealousy.

Nowadays a beautiful yellow rose means friendship, so I am willing to stick to that. Friendship.

It is always a fascinating feeling to observe insects, visiting flowers. Their friendship began long time ago in prehistoric Era of Dinosaurs. Why they survived, but dinosaurs couldn't even both species lied eggs? More questions than answers.

Another hardworking gardeners' friend. Tadah!
I know this bug's name! It is a bumblebee
pollinating a cornflower and collecting pollen, and
nectar for its babies. Later she will make honey and
beebread for the winter hibernation time.
It is amazing how they manage to survive elements.

My interest in insects doesn't stop there. I love to illustrate them for colouring and I paint them too. Look, there is the most exciting moth. Made in acrylics on canvas. What a fantastic creature of Mother Nature! Garden Tiger (Arctia caja).

First time I saw it in the potato field and I felt in love with it immediately. I can imagine many scenes of its life, more likely absolutely out of reality, but that's OK. I am sure, it doesn't mind.

Back to roses. Yes, I love to make art of many things, creatures and events. Did you know that Unicorns have a very spoiled diet? They fancy just and only blue roses for breakfast.

Am I out of reality again? Sorry... That's my fate, to be an artist and to see wonders, magic and mystery everywhere. It is known that blue roses are not found in nature...yet... but some experts managed to produce them by some tricky ways.

Good luck with that, however, Unicorns want all things natural.

In my opinion clouds are flowers too, aren't they?

However, when the Sun plays with fading away drizzle, the wonder happens and sometimes it is very, very close indeed. Is the Leprechaun's pot full with golden coins there... hidden in the chimney?

The most fascinating photo of the Moon in my photo collection is the Super Moon.
No, it is not made by Photoshop.
Yes, all dimensions are real.
Yes, I cropped that pic a bit.
I am very privileged to live in a high-rise flat with a view to the East.
Yes, with a view to die for.
Yes, it is my forever home.
No, aircrafts' noise doesn't bother me at all.
I love to watch their take-offs and landings.
Aircrafts are like big birds.

Yes, I love birds.
Yes, I have some photos of birds.

One beautiful and hot summer's day a runaway
parrot visited me and it was glad to allow me to
grab a camera and take a couple of shots.
Thank you little beauty.
Thank you for patience to pose for my photo

collection.
You made my day.

My love to birds is endless and I have some illustrations of them in my colouring books.

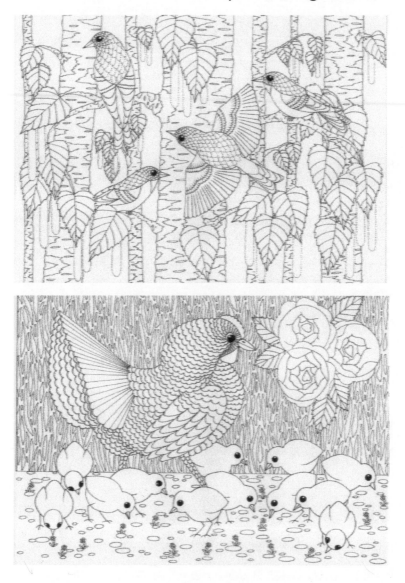

Which do you prefer? Bramblings or Chickens?
Both? That's great! I love them all. Happy colouring!

When I bought a little climbing plant in our local garden shop, I didn't know anything about it, so a battle with it began. It was growing fast, climbed high, flowered beautifully and even produced a fruit.

Aha, you know its name – Passion Flower.

Passion Fruit.

Later it became yellow and was quite delicious.
I can't wait for next year.
Maybe it will produce some more fruit.
It is said that Passion Flower tea could help to sleep better and lower blood pressure.
No, I didn't try Passion Flower tea yet.

Yes, I sleep well, especially after I spend some hours writing or painting. The brain needs some rest.

I can whisper you a little secret.
This is a communal garden where I am honoured to do what I want.

We all are 3rd youth age residents here and I have a couple of lovely friends who are able to work in the garden, so it is a bit egoistic to say that it is just my garden.

However, most of residents are happy to come down, sit in the garden in sunshine and even to collect some money for new plants or garden equipment.

Big, big thank you for that.

They even managed to make a big surprise for me.

One day I was asked what my favourite plant is.
I didn't hesitate to confess that I am dreaming for a palm tree...
And, do you know what? They put together some money and bought 2 (two!) palm trees for me and our garden!

I feel very blessed to live among so many good, loving and caring people.

I call it "Happiness in the Pot".

.

Its beautifully spotted stem and strange, sharply pointed, big leaves wondered anybody who looked at it, but nobody knew its name nor where it came from. It was so weird that some friends called it, the Devil's Plant, Evil looking Weed or Wicked Twig.

Luckily we live in the Technical Era with access to the Internet. I found very little information about this alien plant, however it is named as...

Woodoo Lily.

Hmmm... Even botanists, who named it, found its appearance a bit strange and monsterous.

Weird, Evil or Wicked, the little and happy Scarecrow doesn't mind to have a chat with a Woodoo Lily. They suit each other very well.

What's this?

You can guess how many times you want, I bet, you will not have any idea.

It is a Woodoo Lily's flower! It appears before the leaf emerges. You can compare it with Calla Lily's flower. The structure is the same, just colours are different and one more difference.
 Woodoo Lily's flower has not any stem. It pours out straight from the ground as a dark, purplish brown 30 to 40 cm (12 to 16 inch) long stick.
A very, very unusual flower indeed and I am happy that it is there, even I'll never know where it came from... but... is that important?

There it is. Woodoo Lily flower's bud. Enjoy.

The tallest lily in the garden is Pretty Woman.
Its waxy flower looks artificial, especially if you
touch its thick petals. Look, how many buds it has
and how gorgeous it is in full flowering time.

Purple Prince and Pineapple Lily give to the garden exotic look and fill up air with glorious scent.

One of most beautiful and hardy flower that works very well for ground covering and low maintenance is Forget-Me-Nots.

And one more important thing. Slugs and snails don't fancy them.
It is a win-win situation for me and the garden.
For slugs and snails? Who cares...

WOW... Easter surprise in the garden! Hmm... what kind of a bird hatchet that rabbit who can lay beautifully marbled eggs?

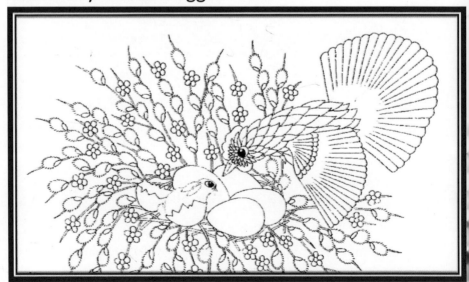

The garden is always work in progress. I am quite relaxed about lawn mowing. I like that there are seen little flowers and I even don't mind some dandelions because every green leaf produces oxygen, purifies air from carbon dioxide and flowers have nectar and pollen for bees and butterflies.

When I cut short this oriental Japanese Willow, my friends called me "hooligan" and "destroyer", and laughed, and made silly jokes about my "green fingers". Then we waited for summer to see what will happen with that poor tree. Even I was not prepared to see so huge regrow. What next?

A communal garden has its advantages. It is always an object of wishes, jokes, surprises and creations. Summers had hot days and we were dreaming about a swimming pool. Ok, if people want a swimming pool I can make one...

Tadah! There it is!
With a nice fountain surrounded by Fuchsias, Fairies and a hiding Fox...
What? Isn't it big enough?
Sorry guys, I'll try again next year...

Some little plastic creatures enjoy my swimming pool very much.
Yes, it is just a 20 litres plastic box on a table.

There is one very sad story that I can tell you that happened in the garden.

Our garden somehow is positioned on the way of an air tunnel. Any little breeze makes there a mini tornado, so everything must be tied up and secured well.

One night there was a storm and our lovely groom was picked up by a big garden tornado, hit to the ground and smashed in pieces...

Yes, I loved him...

Yes, I miss him very much...

No, I am not going to replace him.

Lesson learned.

Luckily a little greenhouse was secured properly.

The spring is a very exciting time of the year. Everything is coming to life. Seedlings have a good chance to survive cool nights in a greenhouse.

Our garden is more tamed to be a show garden with a big lawn for people to enjoy sunshine, have a chat and relax in beautiful surroundings.

However, we managed to install not only one, but three little greenhouses for peppers, tomatoes and cucumbers.

Home grown vegies taste much better and we enjoy them very much.

I couldn't believe my eyes when I discovered that a huge tomato plant appeared in the Fuchsia's pot. How it could happen? Maybe a little bird made poo in the pot after eating some tomato seeds?

They could be Robins or Magpies. Who knows?

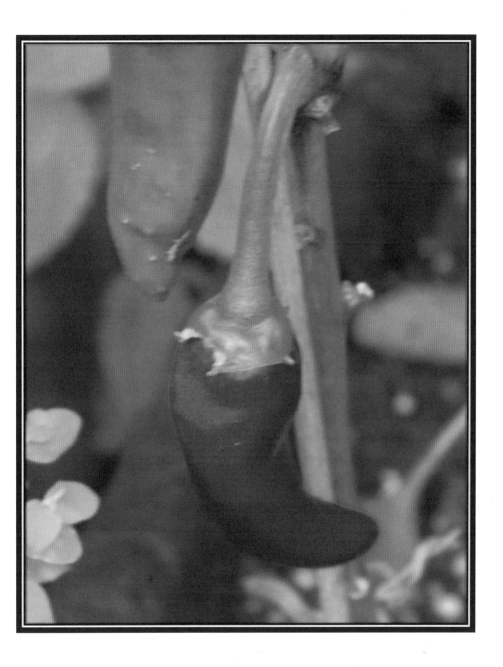

Hot, hot, Red Chilli Pepper is ready to harvest.
I know who will eat it.
No, not me!
My favourite seasoning plant is dill.

I needed to replant this unusual rose, so I didn't expect any flowers in the same summer.

However, it survived very well and, look, it has some beautiful flowers.

Yes, roses are thirsty and hungry plants.

Yes, roses have sharp thorns.

Dark clouds and big seagulls that come inland from the Ocean are warning signs that a monster storm is coming. Pots with decorative plants will be capsized, flowers and leaves broken, and plastic chairs spread all over the garden. It is time to hide them in the shed.

I am resting in my room and waiting for another day when I could go in the garden and check out what kind of disasters happened over the night.
Every morning I expect a spectacular sunrise.
However, more often it looks like this.

It is almost an unreal feeling to see so thick mist. Birds aren't chirping, aircrafts aren't taking off, tree branches aren't moving... silence... scary silence...

I am not giving up hope that there will be a dramatic sunrise for me to enjoy and take photos.

Flowers made of clouds.

Look, look! An Elephant in the swimming pool!
Who said that this swimming pool is too small?

Mysterious monster-weaver is working hard.

There is always something to do in the garden from assembling to digging, and from repairing to watering.

Yes, gardening is labour of love... non-stop...

After all huge efforts in clipping and digging, and watering, and exploring new tools, we could sit down and relax... for a moment, because tomorrow will be a hot day again.

A strong fence is good for our privacy, however, it is useful for hanging baskets too. It is so nice to bring a lot of colours in the garden by so simple way.

Petunias, Lobelias, oriental Grass… everything is growing, flowering and seeding like mad.

Wow... who are you? How you came in the garden?
Are you edible?
No, I'll not try to eat it. Mushrooms is not my
favourite food.

I am glad to introduce to you this beautiful Iris.
What's its name? I don't try to remember.
The label is somewhere in the shed.

After several hot summer days it is raining again.
It is good for anybody.
Air is fresh for breathing, soil is soaked with moist
and plants can grow in full glory.
And I am happy to spy with my little eye.

Birds, birds and birds everywhere.
My lovely "partner in crime", my camera is always
ready for "hunting". I am sure, we do very well.

Birds' Whisperer. When a little bird lands on your palm, it is so sweet feeling that you'll never forget. You don't feel its weight, just gentle claws' touch and you think that maybe you are dreaming.

After that surreal experience I illustrated this imaginative Dreaming Alien Bird.
However, what if on a far, far away planet lives this beautiful monster? What colour sky is there?

It is not an every day's event that air ambulance lands in the nearest park, or a beautiful military aircraft makes training landing-take-offs.
What a fantastic chance to enjoy their appearance and take some photos.
Why I am taking so many photos?
You know, a picture is worth of thousand words.

The Sun, some water and soil
It is enough for a flower to grow.
The Sun, some water and a flower
It is enough for a butterfly to grow.
The Sun, some flowers and love
It is enough for a Fairy to grow.

To be honest, it is very rare, when those little
monsters allow me to take good photos of them.
When I am without the camera, they are coming,
sitting on my hands, playing their games in flowers
and birds are trying to pet me...
Don't they like a camera?
Or maybe it is because behind the camera my brain
is working in more active frequency than flowers
and insects. I should control that process better.

However, everything is ok when I am painting them.
They are still in my mind and make me happy.

The sunset is colouring clouds over the town.

Flowers and trees are going to sleep.

Good night, good night and see you tomorrow.

A nice cup of tea makes me a good company in the waiting game for this spectacular sunrise. Joy is flowing in my veins and a smile decorates my face.

Big monster cranes are in the kissing position and my little Desert Roses are happy on the windowsill. Yes, another lovely day is ahead.

Good morning Sunshine! Bon Appetite!

This little tour through the garden and sky, and my windowsill is a dedication for my truly friends and "partners in crime" in gardening and life.

Dave & Margaret & Tony.

Thank you for your hard work and support.

Gardeners don't get old, they just go to pot.

Printed in Great Britain
by Amazon

21290327R00040